R. VAUGHAN WILLIAMS

IN THE FEN COUNTRY

Symphonic Impression

Oxford University Press

Music Department, 44 Conduit Street, London, W1R ODE

NOTE

This work was first performed in London in 1909 conducted by Thomas Beecham. The scoring was revised in 1935.

It has been recorded by the New Philharmonia Orchestra conducted by Sir Adrian Boult on ASD-2393 (stereo).

ORCHESTRATION

3 flutes	4 horns
2 oboes	2 trumpets
cor anglais	3 trombones
2 clarinets	tuba
bass clarinet	timpani
2 bassoons	strings

Duration 14 *minutes*

Large-size scores and instrumental parts are on hire.

In The Fen Country

Symphonic Impression

R. Vaughan Williams

 Printed in Great Britain

OXFORD UNIVERSITY PRESS, MUSIC DEPARTMENT, 44 CONDUIT STREET, LONDON, W1R 0DE

C. A.
Cl. I in B♭
Hn. I in F
Solo Vla.
Solo
p espr.
ppp
Solo
p espr.
pp
A
Fl. I
Solo
mp espr.
Ob. I
Solo
p espr.
C. A.
Cl. I in B♭
pp
Bn. I
pp
Hn. I
A
Solo Vln.
senza sord.
p espress.
I
Vlns.
II
con sord.
pp
con sord.
pp
Vla.
Mute on

Fls. I II
I
p espr.
II *p espr.*

Obs. I II
I
p espr.
II *p espr.*

C.A.
p espr.
cue for Ob II
p espr.

Cls. I II
I
Cl. I cue for B.Cl.
mp
p
p

B.Cl.
p espr.

Bns. I II
p espr.

Hns.
I II
II
p
III IV
III Solo
p

Solo Vln.

Vlns.
I
div. by desks
pp
II
div. by desks
pp

Vla.
Tutte con sord.
p espr.
p

Vcl.
(senza sord.)
p espr.

Cb.

Fl.II cue for Fl.III
Solo
Fls.
p
mf
I Solo
mf espr.
Obs.
Solo
cue for Ob.II
C.A.
Soli
Cls. in B♭
mf espr.
B.Cl.
I
Bns.
pp
Hns.
III
Solo Vln.
p espr.
I
Vlns.
II
unis.
div.
Vla.
p espr.
Vcl.
Cb.

B Largamente
poco rit.
fp
f
f
f
pp
p espr.
Cl. II cue for B.Cl.
Solo
p
pp
Solo
f
p
p
p
p
IV
p
B Largamente
poco rit.
1 Desk cue for B.Cl.
p
(Tutti)
p

Poco animato
(♪= 128)
rit.
in C Tempo I° (♪= 112)
Fls.
Obs.
C.A.
Cls.
B Cl.
Bns.
I II
Hns.
III IV
I II
Tbns.
III
Timp.
Poco animato
(♪= 128)
rit.
in C Tempo I° (♪= 112)
Vln.I
div.
Vln. II
unis.
unis.
senza sord.
Vla.
Vcl.
Cb.

a2 Soli
mf
mp
a 2 Soli
mf
Cl.II cue for B.Cl.
mf
mf
I
mp
senza sord.
mp
div. a 4
senza sord.
mp
senza sord.
mp
mf

Fl.II cue for Fl.III
Fl.I cue for Fl.III
Fls.
Obs.
C.A.
Cls.
B.Cl.
Bns.
II.
I
Hns.
III
Tpts.
Vln. I
div. a 4
unis.
div.
unis.
unis.
Vln. II
div. a 2
div.
Vla.
Vcl.
Cb.

D

mf cresc.

f

poco f

8

f

cantando

mf

cantando

a2

poco f

poco f

p

mf cresc.

poco f

p

mf cresc.

cresc.

f

pp

D

8

mf cresc.

f cantando

div.a2

mf cresc.

f cantando

8

mf cresc.

f

poco f

mf cresc.

f

poco f

unis.

mf cresc.

div.

f

unis.

poco f

mf cresc.

f cantando

mf cresc.

poco f

Fls.
f
mf
cresc.
Obs.
mf cresc.
C.A.
mf cresc.
Cls.
mf cresc.
B.Cl.
mf cresc.
Bns.
mf cresc.
Hns.
mf
stopped
f
nat.
pp
mf cresc.
mf cresc.
stopped
Solo
Tpts.
mf
cant.
Tuba
div.
Vln. I
div.
mf
mf
cresc.
cresc.
Vln. II
div.
f cant.
cresc.
div.
f cant.
cresc.
Vla.
f
mf cresc.
Vcl.
mf cresc.
Cb.
mf cresc.
9
8

Largamente
appassionato, dim.
11
a2
ff
f
poco f
f sost.
p cresc.
pp cresc.
unis.
div.
sost.

poco accel.
cresc.
Tempo tranquillo
Fls
Obs.
C.A.
Cls.
a2
B.Cl.
Bns.
Hns.
sost.
Tpts.
Tbns.
Tuba
Timp.
tr
poco accel.
cresc.
Tempo tranquillo
div.
a 3
loco
I
Vlns.
II
unis.
Vla.
Vcl.
Cb.

E
legato
legato
legato
legato
9
8
tr
f
E
unis.
div.
unis
div.
div.

rit.
Fls.
Obs.
C.A.
Cls.
B.Cl.
Bns.
Hns.
Tpts.
Tbns.
Tuba
Timp.
rit.
div.
unis.
div.
I
Vlns.
II
unis.
div.
unis.
Vla.
unis.
div.
Vcl.
Cb.

Poco piu mosso

Molto tranquillo

Fls.
1.
pp
Obs.
1.
pp
pp
C.A.
Cls.
pp
pp
pp
Bns.
pp
I
II
pp
pp
Hns.
Tbns.
Tuba
Soli
p
Timp.
tr
pp
I
Vlns.
II
unis.
pp
div.
pp
pp
Vla.
Vcl.
unis.
pp
Cb.

F

poco rit.

Soli

p

pp

F

poco rit.

unis.

p

Lento (♩ = 58-56)
Fls.
pp
Ob. I
cue for Fl. III
Cls.
Bns.
I
Hns.
fz
bouché
p
pp
Tpt. I
Solo
Tbns.
Timp.
Lento (♩ = 58-56)
I
Vlns.
II
div. a 4
div. a 2
Vla.
sul pont.
Vcl.
Cb.

G
Solo
Ob.I
p dolce e teneramente
Bn.I
Solo
Hn.I
p espr.
G
I
Vlns.
II
pp
unis. nat.
Vla.
div a 2
Vcl.
pp nat.
A tempo (sempre tempo rubato)
Ob.I
Hn.I
p dolce
I
Vlns.
II
div.
unis.
div.
unis.
Vla.
div
unis.
Vcl.
unis.
pp

Ob.1
Cl.1
Solo
p dolce e teneramente
Hn.1
I
Vlns.
II
pp
Vla.
Vcl.
H Poco animando
Fls.
a 2
p misterioso
p misterioso
Cl. 1
Bns.
pp
pp misterioso
Hns. III IV
pp misterioso
I
Vlns
II
div.
unis. sul G
pp
sul G
div.
pp misterioso
Vla.
pp misterioso
Vcl.
Cb.
pp misterioso

Fls.
Ob.I
Solo
p teneramente
C. A.
B.Cl.
pp
Bns.
I (cue for B.Cl.)
pp
p
Hns.
p
pp
I
Vlns.
II
dolciss.
pp
unis.
dolciss.
pp
pp misterioso
div.
Vla.
div.
Vcl.
Solo p
Tutti
pp dolciss.
Cb.
pp misterioso

J I Solo

Fls.
Fl.II cue for Ob.II *f* appass.

I Solo
Obs.
mp teneramente *p* *mf*
Soli
f appass.

C.A.
Solo
mf
mf appass.

Cls.
mf 3 *p* 3
mf appass.

B.Cl.
p cresc. poco *f*

Bns.
mp
Bn I cue for B Cl *p* cresc.
appass.

Hns.
Solo 3 *mf*
3
Solo poco *f*
mf appass.
mf appass.

Tpt.I

J

Vln.I
3 *pp* dolce
div. 3 *mf* espr. *f* appass

Vln.II
pp
Soli *mf* espr.
poco *f* appass.
div.
pp
Soli *mf* espr.

Vla. solo
Solo *mp* espr. 3

Vle. (div.)
div. unis. *mp* cresc. 3
div. *f* appass.

Vcl. solo
mp teneramente
poco *f* appass.

Vcl.
pp cresc.
poco *f* appass.

Cb.
pizz. *pp* cresc.
arco *mf* appass.

22
mf cresc.
Soli
mf appass.
cresc.
II cue for B.Cl.
mf cant.
unis.
appass.
mf cresc.
non div.
Solo
Tutte div.
unis.
mf appass.
Tutti div.
div.
p cresc.
mf cresc.
unis

Largamente
dim.
a2
f appass.
Fls.
Obs.
C.A.
Cls.
B.Cl.
Bns.
Hns.
Tpt.I
Timp.
p
mp
mf
Largamente
dim.
Vln.I
div.
Vln.II
Vle.
Tutte div.
Vcl.
Cb.
f appass.

f dim.
p
pp
p
pp
pp
f
dim.
pp
f
mf dim.
p
pp
pp
f
p
dim.
3
pp
p
pp
pp
pp
pp
f
p
f
pp
3
p
pp

K Poco animando
Fls.
Obs.
C.A.
Solo
Cls.
B.Cl.
Bns.
II cue for B.Cl.
I Solo
Hns.
K Poco animando
Vln. I
div a 4
Vln.II
div a 4
Vla.
div. a 4
Vcl.
div. a 4
1 Desk
Cb.

8
p
Solo
mp
p
mf agitato
mf agitato
mf
I
mf agitato
Solo
mp
mf agitato
unis.
Tutti
p

Fls.
II cue for Fl. III
Obs.
C.A.
Cls.
B.Cl.
Bns.
Hns.
Tpts.
Tbns.
Tuba
unis
Vln. I
unis
Vln. II
unis.
unis.
Vla.
unis.
unis.
unis.
Vcl.
Cb.

L cresc.

pp

cue for Ob.II

a2

cresc.

nat.

L

cresc.

div.

Tempo I° (Largamente)
M
Fls.
Obs.
I
C.A.
ff pesante
Cls.
pesante
ff
B.Cl.
ff pesante
Bns.
ff pesante
a2
Hns.
pesante
Tpts.
Tbns.
Tuba
Timp.
Tempo I° (Largamente)
M
div.
Vln. I
ff cantando
Vln. II
ff cantando
non div.
unis
Vla.
non div.
div.
Vcl.
ff pesante
Cb.
ff pesante

ff
p
mf
cantabile
(tr)
pp
unis
non div.
div.
mf cantabile

Ob. I
C.A.
Cl. II
Bns.
Hns.
Tpt. I
Timp.
I
Vlns.
II
Vla.
Vcl.
Cb
Solo
p
(Muta F in G, E♭ in D
div.
div
pp
3

N
Tempo I° ma poco animato
Solo
mp espr.
II
p
6
8
I Solo
mp espr.
Solo
pp
N
Tempo I° ma poco animato
div.
con sord.
p
div. con sord.
p
unis.
più p
più p
più p
più p
più p

Cl. I
B. Cl.
Bns.
Hns.
I
Vlns.
II
Vcl.
Solo
mp espr.
Solo
p espr.
p espr
II cue for B. Cl.
con sord.
p espr.
O
C.A.
Cl. I
B Cl.
Bns.
Hns.
Solo Violin
I
Vlns.
II
Vla.
Vcl.
Solo
p espr.
I Solo
p espr.
ppp
I Solo
p espr.
II pp
IV pp
O senza sord.
pp espr.
unis.
pp
dim.
pp
con sord.
p
pp
pp

Ob. I
Solo
pp espr.
C.A.
Hns.
Solo Vln.
I
Vlns.
II
Vla.
legato
Vcl.
div.
pp
Cb.

Largamente
P Poco animato
Fl. I cue for Fl. III
Fls.
Ob. I
Cls.
B.Cl.
I cue for B.Cl.
Bns.
Hns.
pp tranquillo
Tpts.
p tranquillo
Tbns.
Tuba
p tranq.
Timp.
ppp
Largamente
P Poco animato
con sord.
col Tutti
Solo Vln.
I
Vlns.
II
Vla.
unis.
Vcl.
con sord.
Cb.

pp
pp
pp
p dim.
dim. sempre
p dim.
dim.sempre
p dim.
dim. sempre
p dim.
dim sempre
div.
p tranquillo
unis.
p dim.
p tranquillo
p dim.
div: a 3
p tranquillo
p
dim. sempre
div. a 3
p tranquillo
p
dim. sempre

rit.
in Tempo I°
Fls.
ppp
Cls.
B.Cl.
Bns.
Hns.
cue for Fl. III
pp
dim. sempre
Tbns.
Tuba
Timp.
tr
rit.
in Tempo I°
I
Vlns.
II
Vla.
unis.
pp espr.
Vcl.
Cb.
9
8

Composed April 1904
Revised 1905 and 1907
Orchestration revised 1935